It was autumn. The leaves were falling from the trees. The wind was blowing them all around the farmyard. They were in big piles by the wall.

Jelly was walking next to the wall. She was watching two little birds. She could not take her eyes off them. All of a sudden, there was a noise. "Grrr … grrr."

The two little birds flew away. Jelly looked down. "Grrr ... grrr." The noise was coming from a pile of autumn leaves. Jelly was cross because the noise had frightened the birds away.

She moved the pile of leaves with her paw. She saw a nose. Then she saw another nose. "GRRR ... GRRR." Then she saw two balls of spikes.

They were two big hedgehogs. They were talking to each other as they made a home for the winter. They were cross with Jelly because she had disturbed them.

Jelly left them alone. She walked across the autumn leaves slowly. She was looking for more birds. All of a sudden she cried, "meow, meow."

She looked down. She saw a little ball of spikes. It was a little hedgehog. She had trodden on it. Some of its spikes were caught in her paw.

"Rrr … rrr," called the little hedgehog. Jelly had hurt it. It needed help. The two big hedgehogs looked out from their pile of autumn leaves by the wall.

The hedgehogs were cross, because Jelly had trodden on their daughter. She had hurt their daughter! They started to run across the grass towards her.

Jelly ran to the wall. She jumped on it. She was safe! Soon the little hedgehog felt better. Jelly watched mum and dad take her home. Jelly did not walk on the autumn leaves again.

"au"

autumn   caught

because   daughter

"alk"

talking   walking

walk   walked

"all"

all   ball

wall   called

falling